D1738867

HI THERE!
IF YOU ENJOYED THIS COLORING BOOK,
PLEASE HELP US OUT BY LEAVING A
REVIEW ON AMAZON. JUST A SIMPLE
REVIEW WILL MEAN A LOT TO US.
THANK YOU! :)

Onda Flipside Press

COLOR TEST PAGE

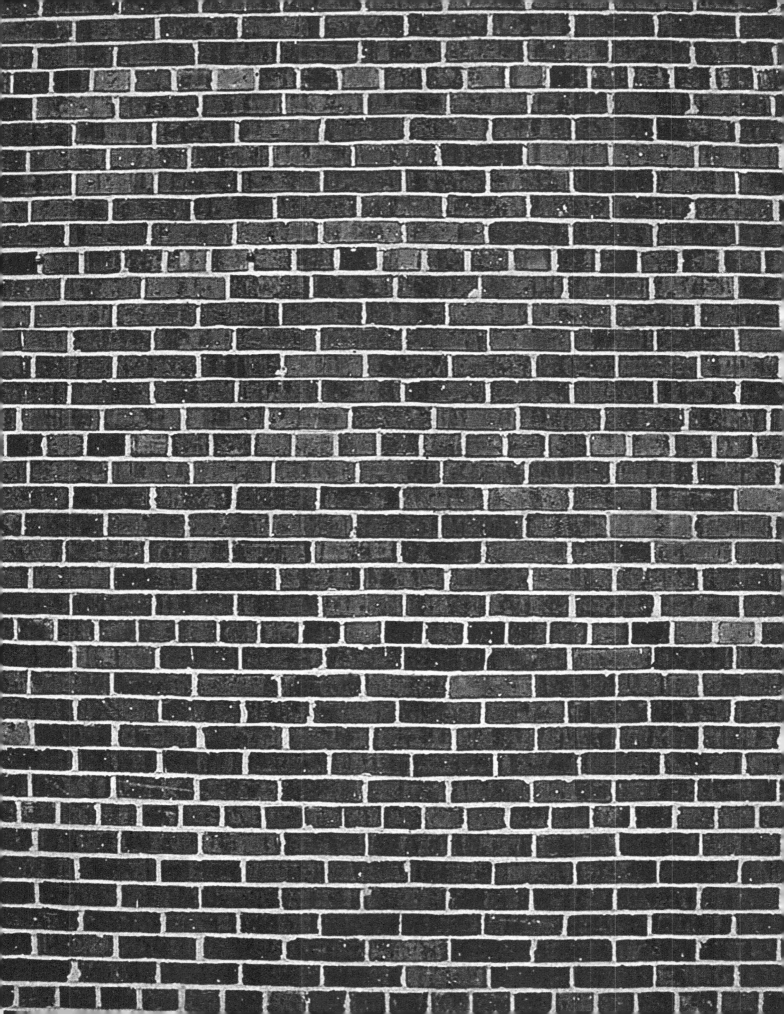

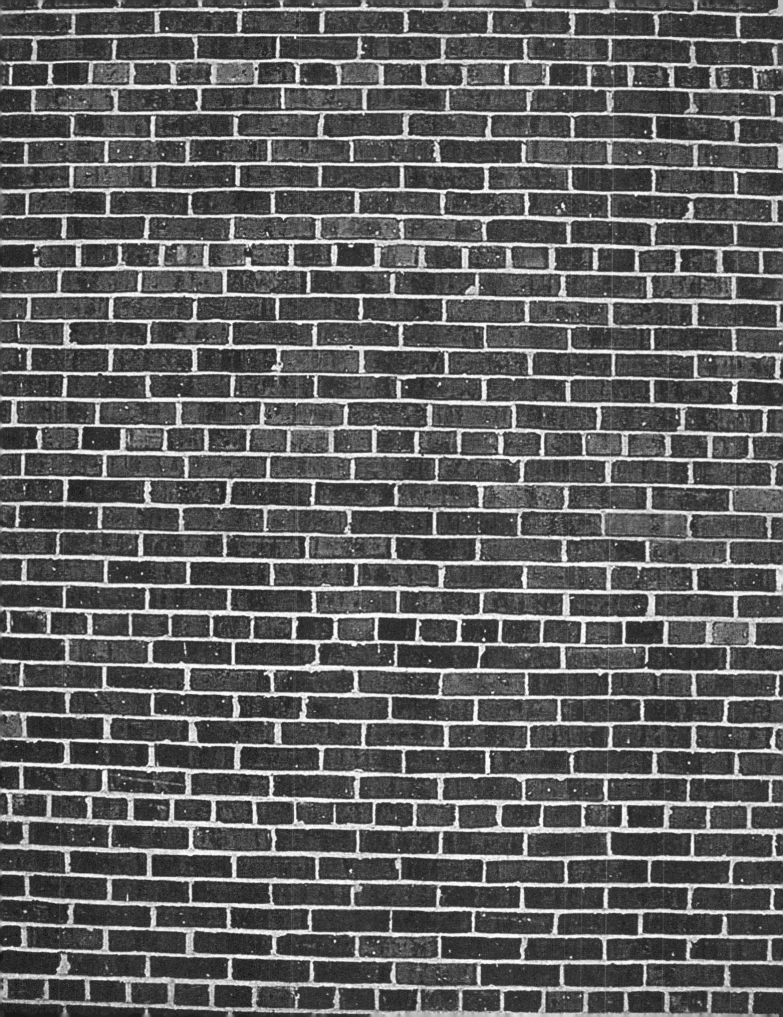

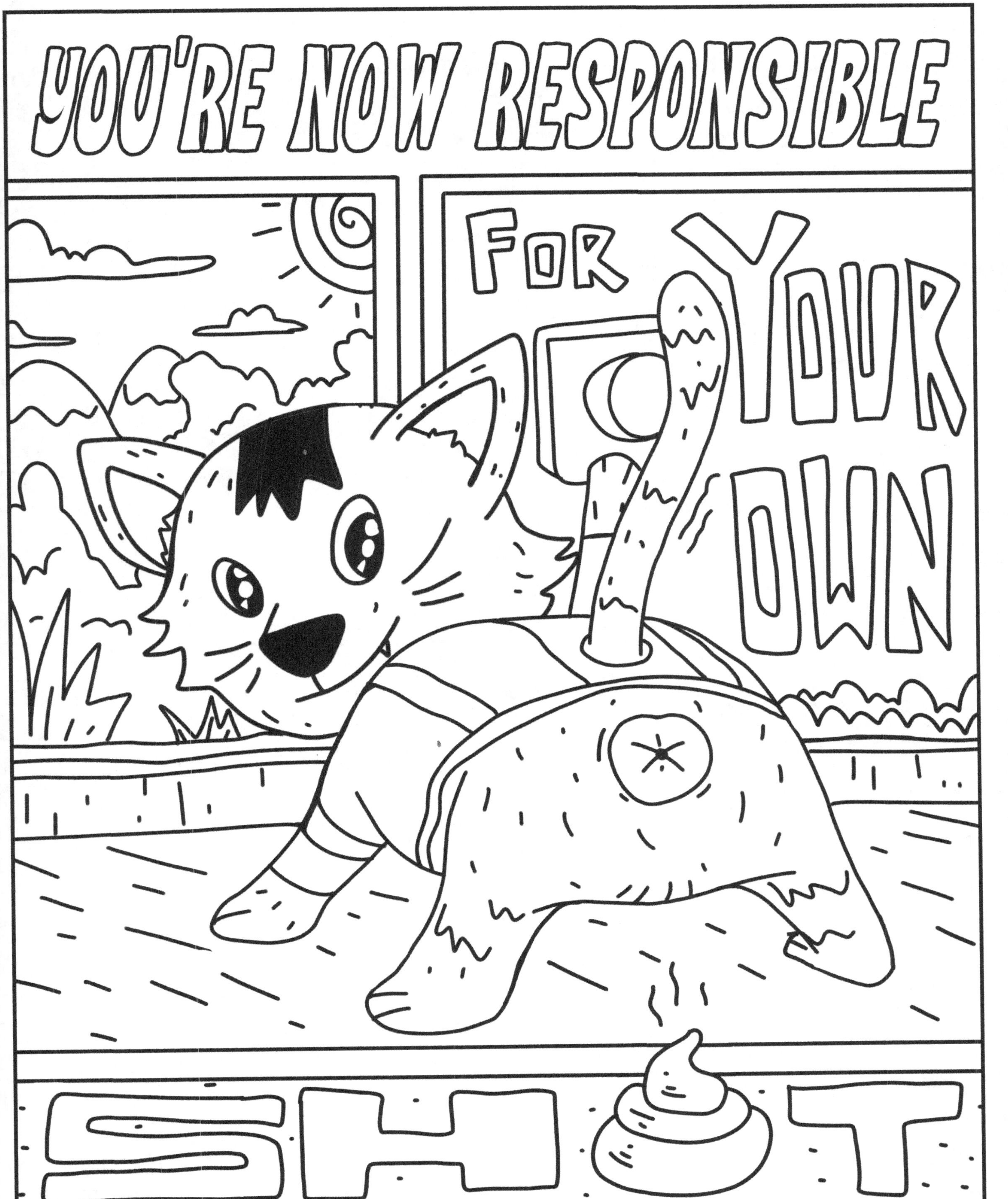
YOU'RE NOW RESPONSIBLE
FOR YOUR OWN
SH T

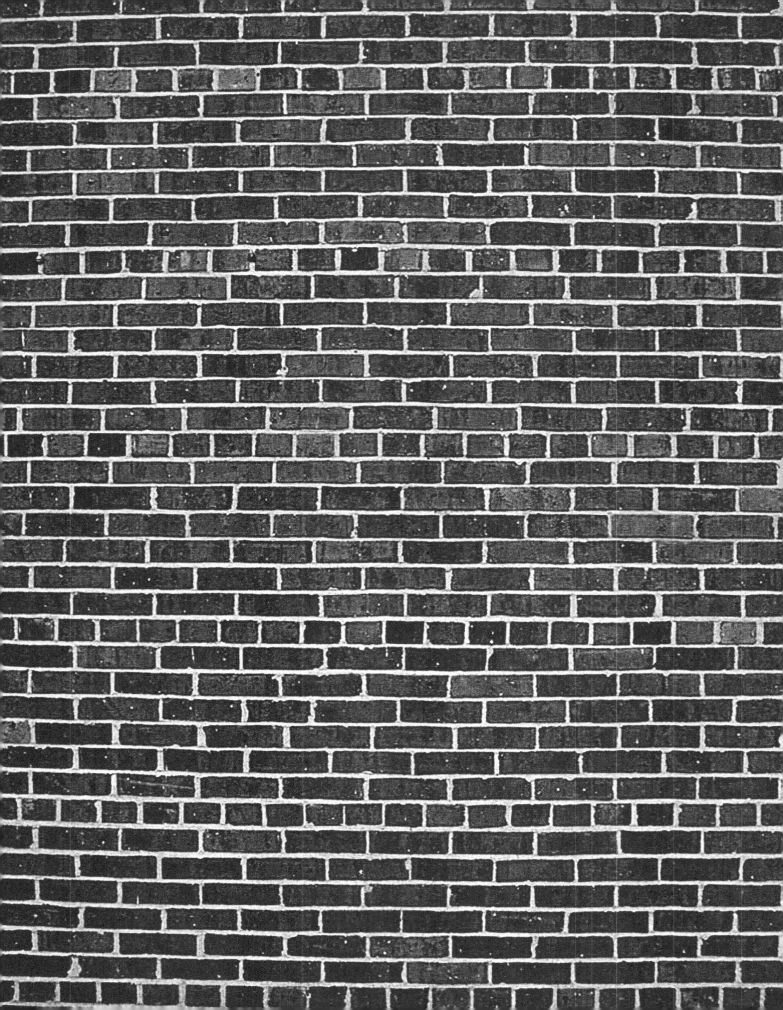

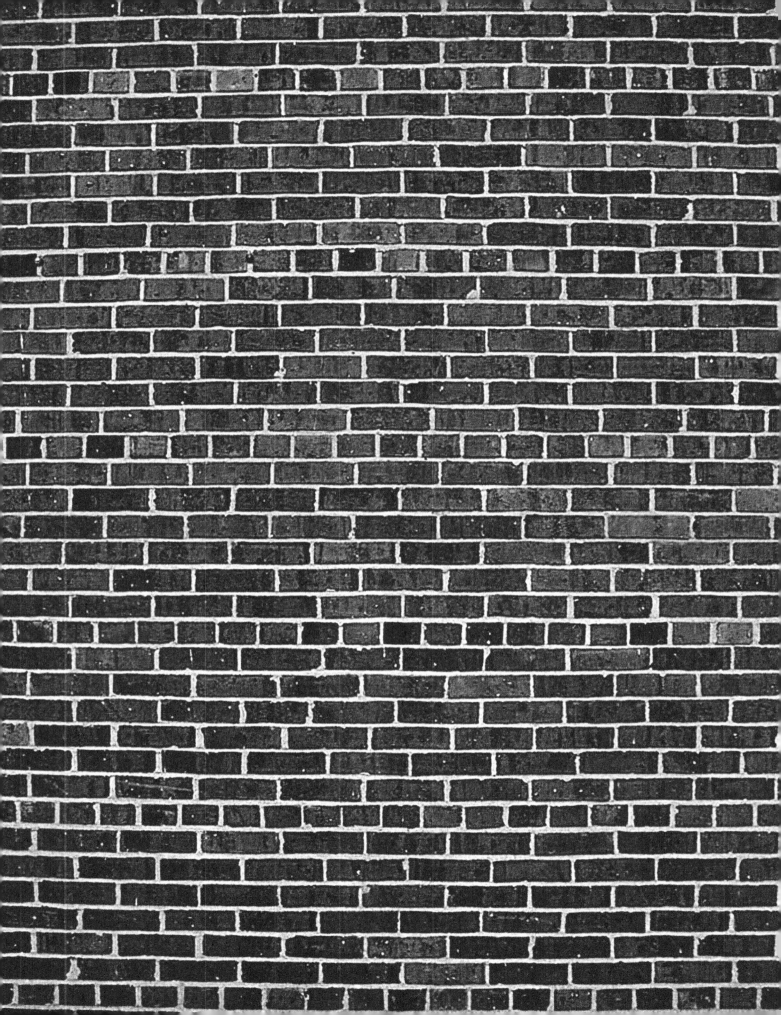

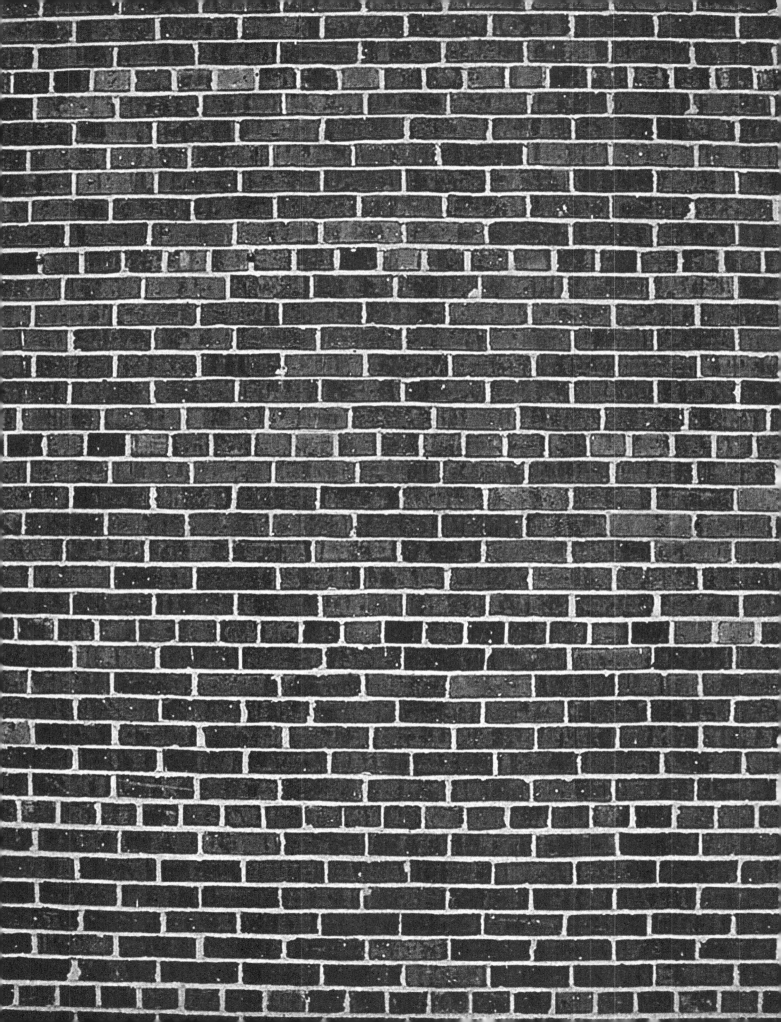

MAZE #01: HELP THE 18-YEAR-OLD KID FIND THEIR PLACE IN THE WORLD

YIPPEE

MAZE #02: HELP THE 18-YEAR-OLD KID GET BACK THEIR CHILDHOOD

MAZE #03: HELP THE 18-YEAR-OLD KID FIND INNER PEACE

MAZE #05: HELP THE 18-YEAR-OLD KID ESCAPE ADULTHOOD

MAZE #06: HELP THE 18-YEAR-OLD KID FIND THEIR OWN PATH

MAZE #07: HELP THE 18-YEAR-OLD KID DISCOVER THEIR PASSIONS

MAZE #08: HELP THE 18-YEAR-OLD KID FIND THEIR PURPOSE IN LIFE

ANSWER KEY

MAZE #01

MAZE #02

MAZE #03

MAZE #04

ANSWER KEY

MAZE #05

MAZE #06

MAZE #07

MAZE #08

Made in the USA
Las Vegas, NV
09 November 2023

80536722R00037